JOHN MUIR

America's First Environmentalist

JOHN MUIR

For Daisy

S. F.

First edition 2006
Library of Congress Cataloging-in-Publication Data is available.
Library of Congress Catalog Card 2005050189
ISBN-13: 978-0-7636-1957-2
ISBN-10: 0-7636-1957-4
2 4 6 8 10 9 7 5 3

Printed in China   This book was typeset in Optima and Interlude.   The illustrations were done in acrylic on paper.

Candlewick Press   2067 Massachusetts Avenue   Cambridge, Massachusetts 02140
visit us at www.candlewick.com

America's First Environmentalist

by Kathryn Lasky

illustrated by Stan Fellows

CANDLEWICK PRESS
CAMBRIDGE, MASSACHUSETTS

Contents

Scotland, 1838–1848

John Muir was wild. His last name, Muir, means "wild land," or "moor," in Scottish. And John was born in Scotland, a wild country with mountains and ruined castles to climb and untamed land to explore.

His favorite pastime was a *scootcher,* what he and his younger brother, David, called a dangerous stunt or a dare. One of their favorite scootchers was to climb out their bedroom window and hang from the windowsill in their nightshirts.

But then John decided to make it harder, more daring. He scootched himself to do it with one hand. David was impressed. So he did the same. John thought he'd better make it even harder. He hung by one finger. But David did that too. So now John decided to climb the very steepest part of the roof and straddle its peak.

The wind was blowing fiercely by the time John reached the peak. His nightshirt billowed out. He hung on tight, as if he were riding a wild horse, and the wind bucked around him. Of course, David had to have a turn at this scootcher too. But his little brother froze and began to cry with fear. "I canna get doon," he whimpered.

John was fearful that if their father discovered them, he would beat them. So he leaned out the window as far as he could and guided his brother's feet down within his own reach, then dragged him back inside by his heels.

But John's father could not follow his daring boys everywhere. He had a store to keep, bills to pay, customers to please. The store was in the house, and beyond that house lay a wilderness—away from the eyes of a stern parent. And it was in the wilderness, looking for songbirds and foxes' dens, that John most loved to be.

The songbirds were among John's favorite creatures. When he came across a lark in its grass nest hidden in the meadow, the bird would shoot straight up into the sky as high as fifty feet and, while treading air with its rapid wing beats, "pour down the most delicious melody."

John admitted that he and his friends sometimes captured a lark and put it in a cage because they loved its song so much. They would even line the bottom of its cage with the same kind of grass and sod as that of the meadow. "Again and again it would try to hover over the miniature meadow from its miniature sky underneath the top of the cage," John wrote later.

But at last, realizing their cruelty, the boys would set it free. "Our great reward was to see it fly and sing in the sky."

John Muir later wrote that the best lessons he was to learn were those learned in "wildness," by which he meant the natural outdoor world. But there was a price if the boys were late or caught missing school, usually a severe thrashing from their father. John's father, however, considered himself a religious man, and so he never beat them on Sundays. His father also liked them to study— school lessons and the Bible. John's father gave him a penny for every Bible verse he learned by heart. John liked money, but he liked adventure more.

VEERY

LESSER SCAUP

CARDINAL

NUTHATCH

RED-WINGED BLACKBIRD

GREAT HORNED OWL

America, 1849

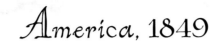

"Bairns," John's father announced one evening, "you needn't learn your lessons tonight, for we're going to America in the morn." He had decided to become a farmer.

John and David had read about America, which to them seemed a "wonder-filled country" with unimaginably high mountains and curious sugar trees from which sweet sap poured.

The land Daniel Muir had bought was in Wisconsin, and the family named their farm Fountain Lake. John called the land "pure wildness."

There were birds for every season. Tiny birds such as chickadees and nuthatches defied the frost and blizzards and stayed through the winter. The loons returned just before spring, when the ice began to melt on the lake. Then the first of the little bluebirds followed. In the summer, the woods were thick with the music of songbirds. And in the fall, the Canada geese honked overhead as they flew south in V-shaped flocks.

EASTERN BLUEBIRD

GREAT BLUE HERON

CANVASBACK

COMMON LOON

The boys did not go to school but were forced by their father to work sixteen-hour days, clearing the wilderness, plowing the fields, and making the land into a productive farm. But even though his waking hours were consumed with such tasks as chopping wood and digging wells, John was never too busy to notice with wonder and delight the creatures and flowers, the stars, and the sounds of this new land.

One winter night, he stood in a snowy field and watched the long rays of colored light stream down from above and rake the sky with their trembling motions. In Scotland these lights had been called the Merry Dancers, but here they were called the Aurora Borealis. And unlike in Scotland, where they were simply pale yellow or white, in this new country the sky folded with shades of crimson and purple and shimmering gold. Their father cried out to them, "Come, bairns, and see the glory of God!" And John Muir stood transfixed by these divine inventions that swept across the Wisconsin night.

Between chasing creatures and watching stars, John began to miss school and book learning. He asked his father to buy him some books on mathematics. Within a summer, he had mastered everything in the first book and then went on to teach himself algebra, geometry, and trigonometry. Secretly he read novels, which his father, who read only the Bible, disapproved of. Soon his father felt John was staying up too late with his books. He said that if John wanted to study, he would have to get up early in the morning.

So John rose the next morning at one hour after midnight. He was so excited with his "five huge, solid hours" before work that he decided to do something more than just read. He decided to invent things.

He went to the cellar, where the tools were kept, and began working on a special sawmill that he had been thinking about. First he made a model and tinkered until he had perfected it. Then he built the sawmill to size and installed it in a creek he had dammed up. It worked: by using the waterpower of the creek, the sawmill could cut logs into a series of even planks while they floated downstream.

This invention was followed by others: a new kind of thermometer, special locks and latches, a barometer, and another device that could measure not only temperature and atmospheric pressure but also the amount of moisture in the air. Perhaps his most beautiful invention was a "star clock." Its long slender hand had a star at the end, which rose and fell with the rising and setting of the sun every day of the year. He accomplished all this in the frosty hours between midnight and dawn.

But it was still what he called "the inventions of God" that interested him most. And if he had a spare moment between inventing and farm chores, he would wander the woods and fields.

Near a pond rimmed with water lilies, there was a meadow that quivered with life—bees buzzing, butterflies fluttering, and wildflowers of every color trembling in the breezes. John loved this meadow so much that he seemed not to mind the mosquitoes and other pesky insects that it harbored in summer. With good humor, he wrote of how much the biting and "stinging pests" savored the taste of boys and girls full of "lively red blood . . . cool from Scotland."

He fell so deeply and passionately in love with this meadow that he began to hope and imagine that some land, land like this meadow, should never be touched or changed or disturbed in any way.

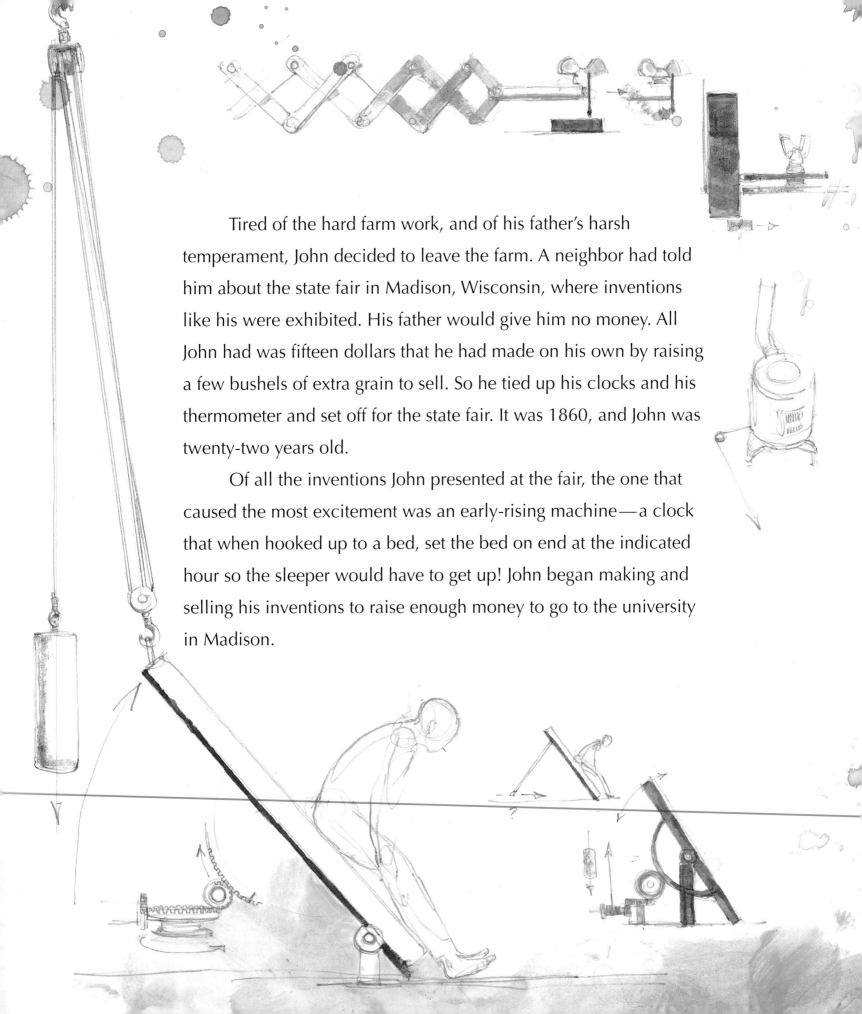

Tired of the hard farm work, and of his father's harsh temperament, John decided to leave the farm. A neighbor had told him about the state fair in Madison, Wisconsin, where inventions like his were exhibited. His father would give him no money. All John had was fifteen dollars that he had made on his own by raising a few bushels of extra grain to sell. So he tied up his clocks and his thermometer and set off for the state fair. It was 1860, and John was twenty-two years old.

Of all the inventions John presented at the fair, the one that caused the most excitement was an early-rising machine—a clock that when hooked up to a bed, set the bed on end at the indicated hour so the sleeper would have to get up! John began making and selling his inventions to raise enough money to go to the university in Madison.

Although he had not been in a real school since he was eleven, John had not fallen behind. He was mostly interested in studying the sciences. But he also studied Latin.

He invented a studying machine to help him. It was a desk in which the books were arranged in a certain order at the beginning of each term. When his bed–alarm clock set him on his feet to wake him up, it also lit the lamp. Then after a few minutes had passed, enough to allow him to dress, there was another click, and the first book to be studied was pushed up from a rack in the desk and thrown open for John to begin reading.

John spent four years at the university. Just as he was completing his studies, the Civil War broke out. Men were being drafted to fight. John wanted no part of any war. The thought of killing another human being, no matter what the cause, was simply unthinkable.

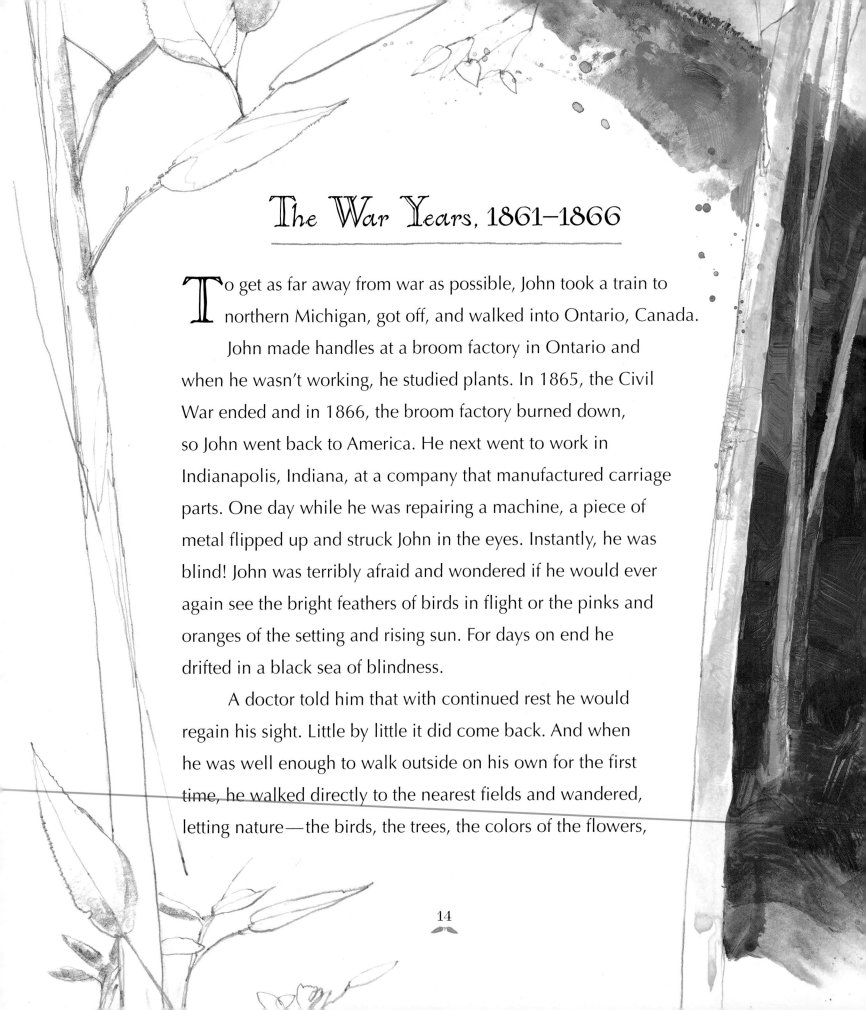

The War Years, 1861–1866

To get as far away from war as possible, John took a train to northern Michigan, got off, and walked into Ontario, Canada. John made handles at a broom factory in Ontario and when he wasn't working, he studied plants. In 1865, the Civil War ended and in 1866, the broom factory burned down, so John went back to America. He next went to work in Indianapolis, Indiana, at a company that manufactured carriage parts. One day while he was repairing a machine, a piece of metal flipped up and struck John in the eyes. Instantly, he was blind! John was terribly afraid and wondered if he would ever again see the bright feathers of birds in flight or the pinks and oranges of the setting and rising sun. For days on end he drifted in a black sea of blindness.

A doctor told him that with continued rest he would regain his sight. Little by little it did come back. And when he was well enough to walk outside on his own for the first time, he walked directly to the nearest fields and wandered, letting nature—the birds, the trees, the colors of the flowers,

the fleecy clouds racing across the sky—pour back into him. It was like water for a man dying of thirst.

When he returned to his lodgings that day, he had learned another lesson from nature: the machines he had invented were nothing in comparison to the wilderness. It was wilderness he loved most of all, and now that he could see it again, he wanted to see more of it. He quit his job, took the train to Jeffersonville, Indiana, and began to walk. It was the beginning of a journey that would take him one thousand miles.

Journey to Florida, 1867

Here is what John Muir took with him in a small rubber bag for his thousand-mile walk to the Gulf Coast of Florida: one change of underwear, a comb, a towel, soap, a small device to press samples of plants and leaves, a brush, three books, and a notebook. On the first page he wrote: *John Muir, Earth-planet, Universe.*

John Muir's plan was to go by the "wildest, leafiest, and least trodden way." He rambled through the great oak forests of Kentucky, poked into immense caves, and made his way through a vast grove of giant sunflowers. He covered as much as twenty-five miles a day and crossed two mountain ranges. His eyes, once damaged, grew keener at the sight of each new leaf, animal, and flower.

Five weeks after John had set off, he reached Savannah, Georgia, almost starving and with only twenty-five cents in his pocket. Even with so little money, he still worried about thieves and decided that the safest place to sleep would be the cemetery.

People were usually afraid of graveyards, imagining they harbored wandering spirits and ghosts. But this graveyard was filled with birdsong and with grand old trees draped in long skeins of silvery moss. John saw flocks of butterflies and several eagles. He found streams of rippling water. And so in this place of the dead, he found more life than he ever thought possible.

GULF FRITILLARY

SNAPPING TURTLE

FLAMINGO

From Georgia, John took a steamship to Fernadina Beach, Florida. Florida was about the strangest place that John Muir had ever seen, but he loved it. "Strange plants, strange winds . . . strange birds," he wrote. It was not an easy country to ramble. The vine-tangled swamps were almost impossible to walk through. But he still found them fascinating as he pushed his way into a watery maze of half-submerged forest, where he constantly expected "to plant my feet on an alligator." The living things that most thrilled John were the palm trees. He had never seen anything like these "smooth pillars rising from the grass, each capped with a sphere of leaves, shining in the sun as bright as a star."

Finally, John caught the fresh scent of the salt breeze. He had reached the sea, the Gulf of Mexico, and almost as soon as he got to the seaside village of Cedar Key, he collapsed in a delirious fever. After wading through the swamplands of central Florida, it was not the alligator that had beaten John Muir but the mosquito. He had contracted malaria. Luckily, the owner of a mill where he had worked for one day took him in, and with his wife, nursed John back to health.

MOTTLED DUCK

California, 1868

When he had recovered, John Muir wanted to go to South America, but there was no ship bound in that direction. Instead he boarded a ship heading for San Francisco, California. He didn't especially like the crowded city, but he did take time to notice that in even the smallest and darkest apartments, people grew flowers in tin cans on their windowsills.

People needed nature, he concluded: they needed woods and they needed meadows, not to use or own but simply as places where they could marvel at God's inventions.

Three days after arriving in San Francisco, John stopped
a carpenter in the street and asked, "What's the quickest way
out of the city?"

"Where do you want to go?" the carpenter replied.

"Anywhere that is wild," John said.

The carpenter pointed him in the direction of the Sierra
Nevada Mountains. This time carrying only a blanket, some flour,
tea, and his journal, John Muir of Earth-planet, Universe, set off,
and once more he was swept up in the thrill of the wilderness.

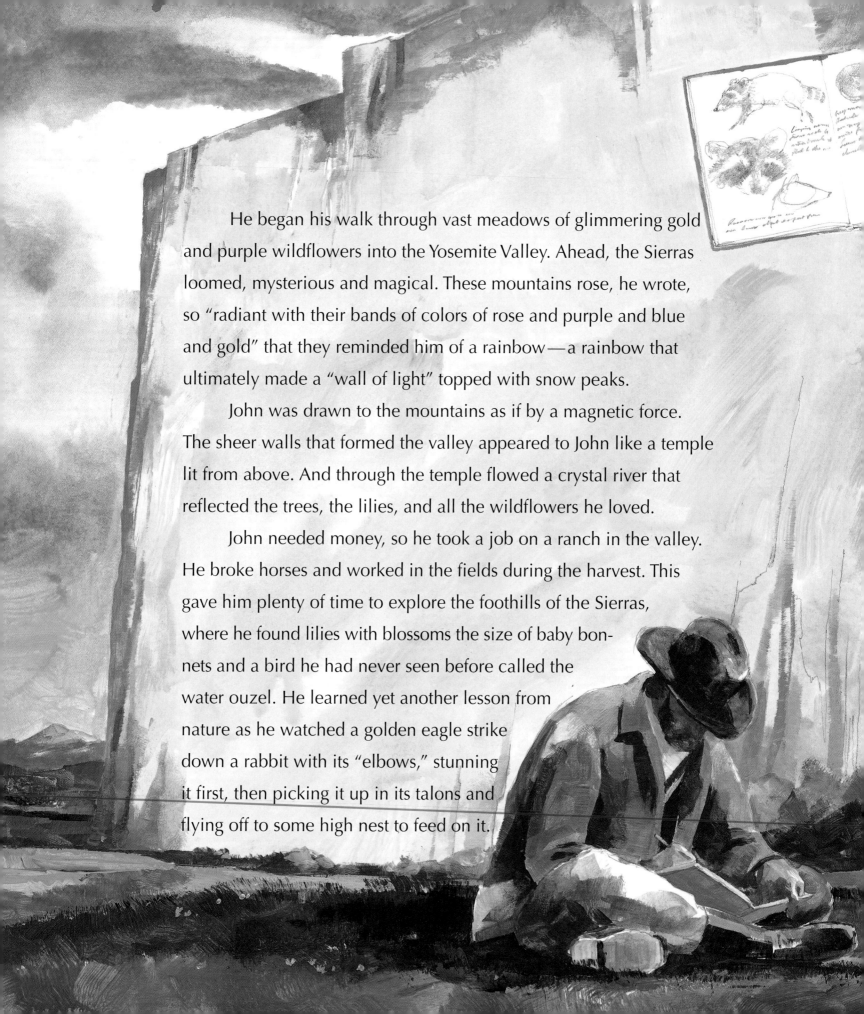

He began his walk through vast meadows of glimmering gold and purple wildflowers into the Yosemite Valley. Ahead, the Sierras loomed, mysterious and magical. These mountains rose, he wrote, so "radiant with their bands of colors of rose and purple and blue and gold" that they reminded him of a rainbow—a rainbow that ultimately made a "wall of light" topped with snow peaks.

John was drawn to the mountains as if by a magnetic force. The sheer walls that formed the valley appeared to John like a temple lit from above. And through the temple flowed a crystal river that reflected the trees, the lilies, and all the wildflowers he loved.

John needed money, so he took a job on a ranch in the valley. He broke horses and worked in the fields during the harvest. This gave him plenty of time to explore the foothills of the Sierras, where he found lilies with blossoms the size of baby bonnets and a bird he had never seen before called the water ouzel. He learned yet another lesson from nature as he watched a golden eagle strike down a rabbit with its "elbows," stunning it first, then picking it up in its talons and flying off to some high nest to feed on it.

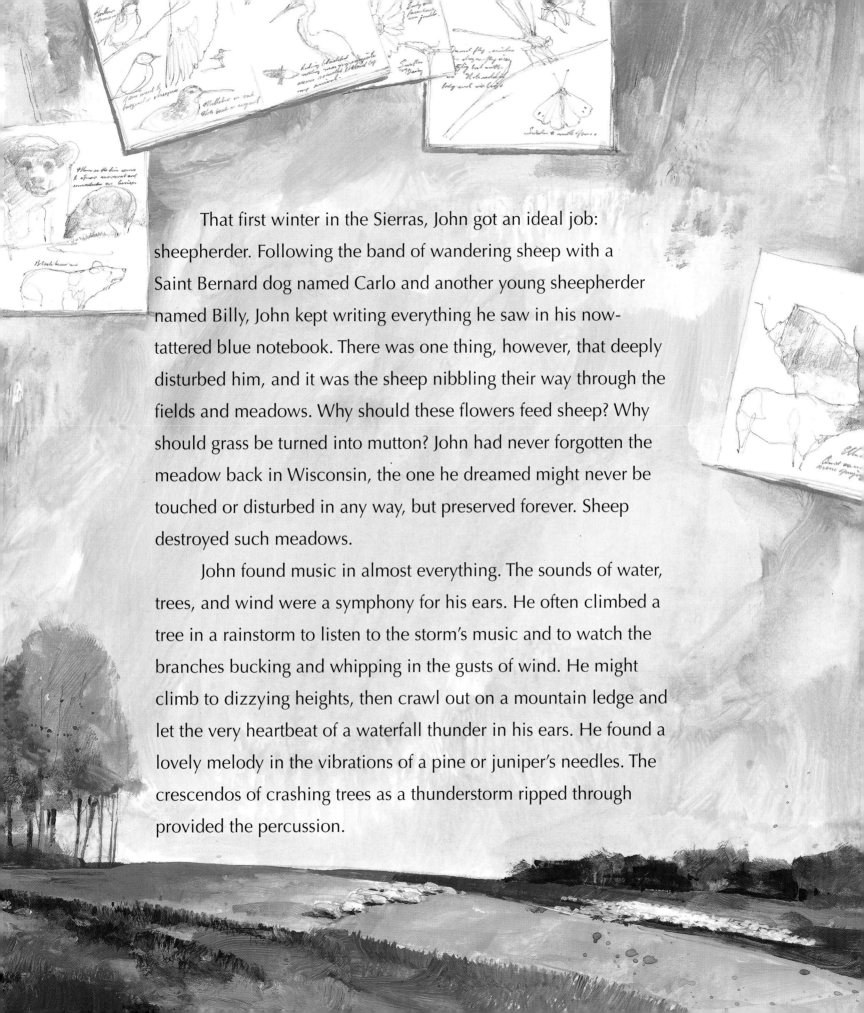

That first winter in the Sierras, John got an ideal job: sheepherder. Following the band of wandering sheep with a Saint Bernard dog named Carlo and another young sheepherder named Billy, John kept writing everything he saw in his now-tattered blue notebook. There was one thing, however, that deeply disturbed him, and it was the sheep nibbling their way through the fields and meadows. Why should these flowers feed sheep? Why should grass be turned into mutton? John had never forgotten the meadow back in Wisconsin, the one he dreamed might never be touched or disturbed in any way, but preserved forever. Sheep destroyed such meadows.

John found music in almost everything. The sounds of water, trees, and wind were a symphony for his ears. He often climbed a tree in a rainstorm to listen to the storm's music and to watch the branches bucking and whipping in the gusts of wind. He might climb to dizzying heights, then crawl out on a mountain ledge and let the very heartbeat of a waterfall thunder in his ears. He found a lovely melody in the vibrations of a pine or juniper's needles. The crescendos of crashing trees as a thunderstorm ripped through provided the percussion.

But it was the mountains that continued to bewitch him. With each job he found, he seemed to move closer to this wall of light.

After he finished herding sheep, he got a job helping to build a sawmill. And when he had finished building the sawmill, he built himself a "hanging nest." It was a box suspended over the stream, strung to the gables of the sawmill. It had two skylights so that he could see South Dome, one of the Sierra peaks, and Yosemite Falls. Cozy in his hanging nest, he would read by candlelight—about plants and animals, rocks and geology, and how the earth had formed and life had begun on the planet that he called home.

It was when John was at the sawmill that he began to make his many climbs into the Sierras, even in the wintertime. He was entranced by snow and ice. He called the six-ray crystals of snow-flakes "snow flowers" and would wade out waist deep in snow to examine these bouquets with his magnifying lens.

John started to do more than observe the secrets of nature. He began to write and to use his writing to help protect the wild places he cherished. He saw that it was not only the grazing sheep that destroyed the meadows of the Sierras. Although he himself had found work at a sawmill, he realized that the forests were being devoured by what he called the "fierce storm of steel." Trees were not only cut, but the immense ones were often dynamited. John began to write vigorous articles warning of the dangers of the timber industry and telling how important it was for people to have "beauty as well as bread, places to play in and pray in, where nature may heal and cheer and give strength to body and soul alike."

What he loved most about winter were the fierce snowstorms that lashed out of the Sierras. So it was not surprising that with his love of snow and blizzards, he would become interested in ice.

Soon his consuming interest was glaciers. John suspected that it was the glaciers that had sculpted the mountains and the Yosemite Valley he loved so much. He imagined that the glaciers, with their slow grinding movement, could have ground down the rock over millions of years, providing places for mosses and flowers to grow.

As diligently as any hunter tracking an animal, John Muir began to track glaciers, for they left their marks. He began his studies in Yosemite by driving stakes into a glacier at intervals in a straight line. A month and a half later, he discovered that indeed the stakes had all moved downhill, one as much as forty-seven inches. Glaciers were alive and moving!

But many important scientists disagreed. They felt that earthquakes were responsible for the sudden changes in the surface of the earth. These men of science had heard of Muir's ideas, but they called him a "mere sheepherder" and even an "ignoramus." John Muir felt that earthquakes could account for many changes, as the scientists said, but not for all. Earthquakes could not cause the valleys to be scooped out or their floors to drop even deeper, nor could they carve mountains.

The glaciers in Yosemite and the Sierras were remnants of ancient ones from the last ice age, which had occurred 12,000 years before. Their tongues of thick ice scraped over mountains like rough sandpaper, leaving polished domes. Glaciers could even rip apart rock and form glacial lakes from their melt. The first article that John Muir ever wrote was about glaciers. Some people thought he might be right. He decided to go to Alaska to learn more.

Alaska, 1879

John went with a group of men and a black dog named Stickeen. The dog was tiny and at first glance appeared helpless. But Stickeen and John became inseparable pals.

One day, John decided to explore a glacier near Taylor Bay. A storm was brewing. John wrote, "I heard the storm and made haste to join it, for many of nature's finest lessons are to be found in her storms."

So he took off with a piece of bread in his pocket and Stickeen at his heels. The storm was a mighty one, and John and Stickeen watched together as rocks splintered from ice crags and broad torrents from swollen mountain streams roared at the glacier's edge. It began to snow. Worried about getting caught in a "tangle of crevasses," deep cracks in the ice that plunged down thousands of feet, John decided they should return to camp.

At first the crevasses were narrow enough to hop across. But they began to grow wider. John would jump and Stickeen would follow. But soon the cracks opened to widths of fifteen, twenty, and thirty feet and were unjumpable. John and Stickeen were caught in a deadly ice maze, and John knew he had to face a "dismal night-dance on the glacier," trying to find his way around these deep cracks. Then they were stopped by the widest crevasse yet—at least forty feet wide. Even worse, John discovered they had accidentally walked onto a narrow island of ice with only two escape routes—one back the way they had come and the other a sunken sliver of ice near the middle of the crevasse that could act as a bridge and get them to the other side. John decided to try the bridge.

He cut steps into the glacier, climbed down them, and then, straddling the bridge, edged out onto it. Beneath him, the ice world dropped away two thousand feet or more. Inching along, he reached the other side and began to carve a new set of steps to climb out. Meanwhile "poor Stickeen, the wee, hairy, sleekit beastie," whimpered at the edge behind him. John tried to coax him down the steps to begin, but for the first time, the dog would not follow.

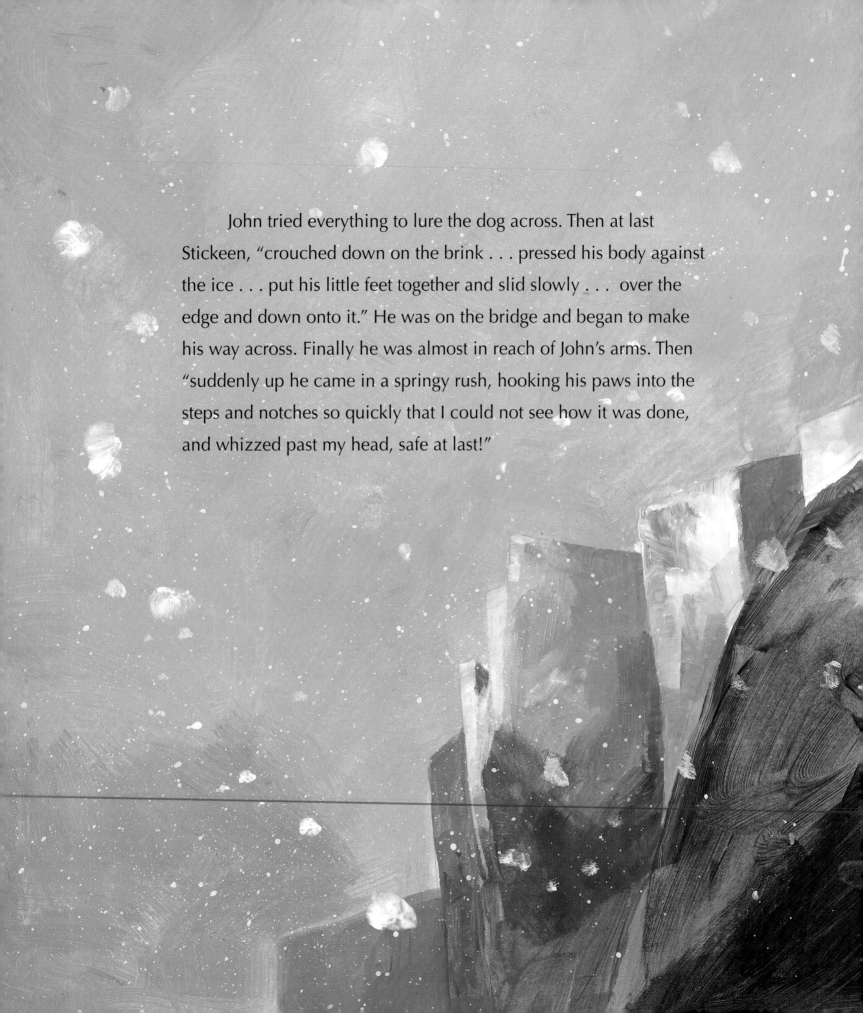

John tried everything to lure the dog across. Then at last
Stickeen, "crouched down on the brink . . . pressed his body against
the ice . . . put his little feet together and slid slowly . . . over the
edge and down onto it." He was on the bridge and began to make
his way across. Finally he was almost in reach of John's arms. Then
"suddenly up he came in a springy rush, hooking his paws into the
steps and notches so quickly that I could not see how it was done,
and whizzed past my head, safe at last!"

Yosemite National Park, 1890

By the time he was forty years old, John Muir had walked tens of thousands of miles, and he would walk more. His clothes had become tattered, his beard more tangled with each year, his face deeply tanned and often covered with soot to shield him from the glare of the sun. He looked as wild as the wilderness he loved.

By the time he was fifty years old, he had decided to devote himself almost completely to writing and the cause of conservation. And finally in 1890, when Muir was fifty-two, his dream came true. A bill was passed and signed by President Benjamin Harrison, and Yosemite National Park was created. Soon there were more parks in California, including Sequoia National Park, where the immense thousand-year-old trees could now continue to grow and give shade in peace.

Still John Muir hiked into his beloved Sierras, often as a personal guide to distinguished Americans.

And while he walked, he often talked. On one such trip, while on horseback with President Theodore Roosevelt, he convinced the president to create a bureau of forestry to manage and protect the trees of forest reserves.

Never a rich man, John nonetheless considered himself a millionaire. In pursuit of wildness, he had found temples of light in mountain valleys, a song in the water of a stream, a symphony in a storm-tossed tree, and snow flowers in a blizzard. Such was the wealth of John Muir, Earth-planet, Universe.

Epilogue

Although John Muir never held public office, he did more to help preserve the American wilderness than any other individual in the country's history. He realized early on the threat overgrazing posed to open lands. He saw how wilderness was being bought up by speculators and corporations, how even water rights were being purchased. He became a spokesman for the land, and his first dream of protecting one single meadow grew into a forceful movement.

In 1892 he founded the Sierra Club to try to build a strong conservation policy and, in particular, to save forests and meadows. He brought his now considerable influence as an environmentalist to politicians. By 1893 the federal government had set aside thirteen million acres for forest reserves. In 1897 a commission recommended that two other national parks—Grand Canyon and Mount Rainier— and additional national forests be created.

Muir wrote constantly and spoke out. He guided many famous Americans, from Ralph Waldo Emerson to Theodore Roosevelt, through his beloved Yosemite Valley. He died in 1914.

Bibliography

FOR FURTHER READING

Douglas, William O. *Muir of the Mountains.* Illustrations by Daniel San Souci. San Francisco: Sierra Club Books for Children, 1994.

SOURCES

The quotations in this book were taken from the following sources:

Muir, John. *Nature Writings.* New York: The Library of America, 1997.
    This collection includes four of Muir's books:
        The Story of My Boyhood and Youth (1913), *My First Summer in the Sierra* (1911), *The Mountains of California* (1894), and *Stickeen* (1909), along with selected essays.
    In addition to quotations from the four books included in the collection, quotations were also taken from these four essays:
        "God's First Temples." *Sacramento Daily Union,* February 5, 1876.
        "Living Glaciers of California." *Harper's Monthly,* November 1875.
        "Snow-Storm on Mount Shasta." *Harper's Monthly,* September 1877.
        "Yosemite Glaciers." *New York Tribune,* December 5, 1871.

———. *Our National Parks.* Boston: Houghton Mifflin, 1901. Reprinted with a foreword by Richard F. Fleck. Madison: University of Wisconsin Press, 1981. Quotations are from the 1981 edition.

———. *A Thousand-Mile Walk to the Gulf.* Edited and with an introduction by William Frederic Badé. Boston: Houghton Mifflin, 1916. Reprinted with an introduction by Peter Jenkins. Boston: Houghton Mifflin/Mariner Books, 1998. Quotations are from the 1998 edition.

About the Sierra Club

John Muir's Sierra Club was founded in 1892 and has grown to more than 750,000 members to date. It is the oldest, largest, and most influential grassroots environmental organization in America. It also became active in Canada in 1963, and the national office of the Sierra Club of Canada was set up in 1989.

The Sierra Club's mission has four parts:

> to explore, enjoy, and protect the wild places of the earth
>
> to practice and promote the responsible use of the earth's ecosystems and resources
>
> to educate and enlist people to protect and restore the quality of the natural and human environment
>
> to use all lawful means to carry out these objectives.

In addition to establishing Yosemite National Park, the Sierra Club helped to establish the Endangered Species Act, which makes it illegal to kill, buy, sell, or trade animals endangered by such factors as loss of habitat or poaching. Because of this act, some species, including the American bald eagle, are no longer under threat of extinction.

In addition to helping to write laws, the Sierra Club also works with youth from all over the country to help them learn about, experience, and speak up for the environment. The organization is committed to preparing youth to inherit the world.

The Sierra Club is always happy to invite children and adults to explore, learn, and take action with them. There are chapters and groups in every state, as well as several international chapters. For more information about the Sierra Club, including how to join, visit www.sierraclub.org or write: The Sierra Club; National Headquarters; 85 Second Street, 2nd Floor; San Francisco, CA 94105.